Brain Training Sight Words 4th – 6th Grade

A Whole Brain Approach to Reading

Bridgette Sharp

Copyright © 2016 Bridgette Sharp
All rights reserved.

Published in the United States of America. No part of this publication may be reproduced, stored in a retrieval system, or transmitted, in any form or by any means: electronic, mechanical photocopying, recording or otherwise, by anyone other than the original purchaser for his or her own personal use without the prior written permission of the publisher.

ISBN-13:
978-1540499547

ISBN-10:
1540499545

Table of Contents

4	What is Brain Training?
5	Introduction
6	Name the Shape
7	Name the Color
8	Name the Number
9	Color and Shape
10	Color and Number
11 - 20	Fourth 100 High Frequency Words
21 - 28	Fifth 100 High Frequency Words
29 - 36	Sixth 100 High Frequency Words

What is Brain Training?

Brain Training consists of many different programs designed to improve brain processing speed, hemispheric integration between the right and left brain, internal brain timing and sequencing.

The exercises in this book are one method of hemispheric integration. While the right brain identifies the color, the left brain is utilized to read the numbers and words. As each exercise is done, the right and left brain must communicate to complete the task. This encourages the neurons to connect. Neurons that fire together wire together. Therefore, the more the exercises are done the stronger the neural connections, the quicker the brain responds.

Pairing brain training with sight words is a natural way to make a difficult task easier. Reading difficulties can often be a result of left brain weakness. Using brain training exercises with sight words engages the right brain to assist with the task. It also benefits the student by improving memory, sequencing and brain processing speed.

The results are often remarkable. Struggling students learn the material quicker and easier. They retain the information and have faster recall, resulting in higher academic achievement, better test scores and school success.

Each exercise begins with reading the words; first very slowly sounding it out and then reading it quickly. Once the student is familiar with the new words, he/she can name the color and then read the word quickly while being timed. You may also choose to do the exercise again reading the word first and then naming the color second. Using a stopwatch, record the time and try to beat it on successive tries.

After reading a grid, have your student use letter tiles to spell the first word on the grid. Then have them write the word on a dry erase board or paper. Do all of the words on that grid. Then read the grid again. This will help with automaticity.

Brain Training grids start at the top left corner and move right across the row. We then move to the row below the one completed and move left to right, continue in this fashion, ending with the bottom right square of the grid. In this example the squares are numbered for you.

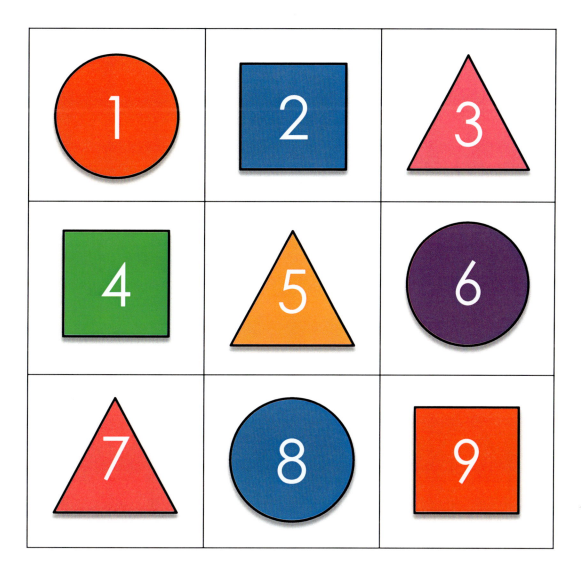

The grids are arranged systematically from simple to more complex, therefore they should be completed in order. Each grid should be done multiple times to assure mastery before moving to the next grid.

Name the Shape. Start at the top left square of the grid and name the shapes. Record your time and try to beat it!

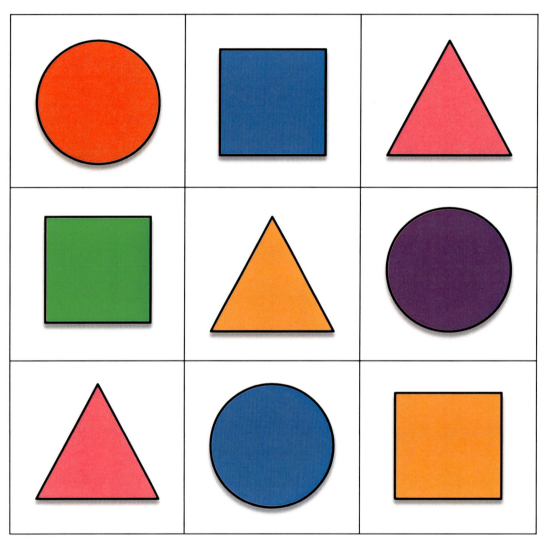

Record your times here!

_____ _____ _____

_____ _____ _____

_____ _____ _____

Name the Color. Start at the top left square of the grid and name the colors. Record your time and try to beat it!

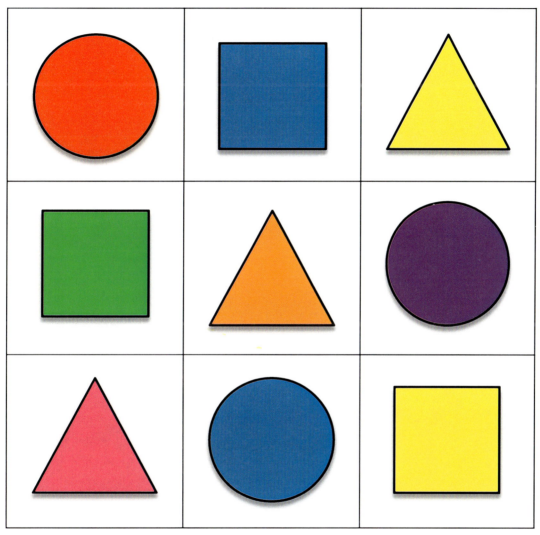

Record your times here!

_____   _____   _____

_____   _____   _____

_____   _____   _____

Name the Number. Start at the top left square of the grid and name the numbers. Record your time and try to beat it!

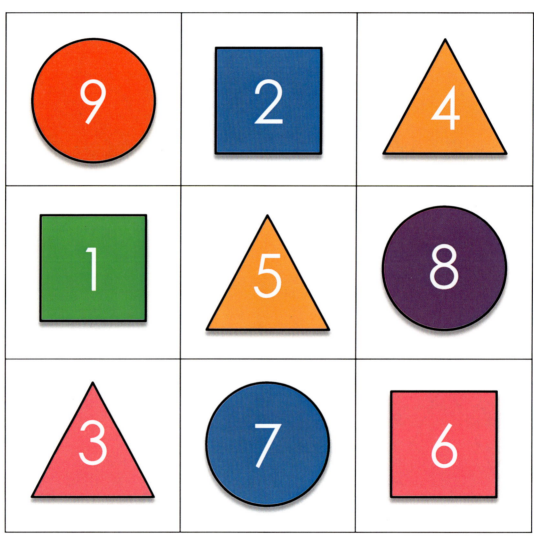

Record your times here!

_____ _____ _____

_____ _____ _____

_____ _____ _____

Name the Color and Shape. Start at the top left square of the grid and name the color first and then the shape.
i.e. "Red Circle" Record your time and try to beat it!

Record your times here!

_____ _____ _____

_____ _____ _____

_____ _____ _____

Name the Color and Number. Start at the top left square of the grid and name the color first and then the number. i.e. "Red Nine" Record your time and try to beat it!

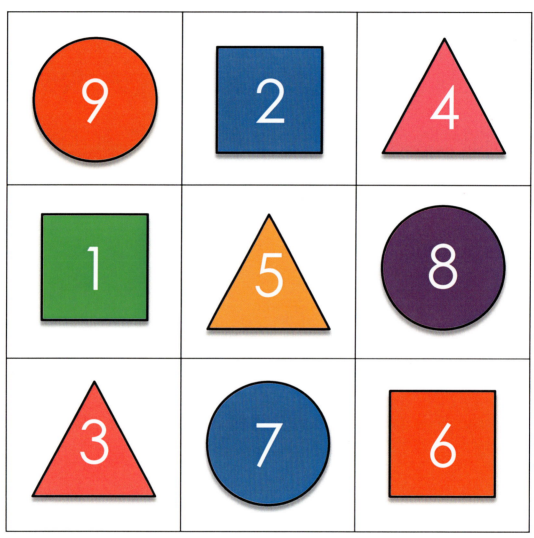

Record your times here!

_____ _____ _____

_____ _____ _____

_____ _____ _____

Read the Words: Start at the first square on the grid and sound out each word very SLOWLY. "Say it slow." Be careful to blend the sounds together. Then say the word quickly. "Say it fast." i.e. "ssssuuunnn, sun…"

Make sure to master these words before proceeding to the next grid. Record your times below.

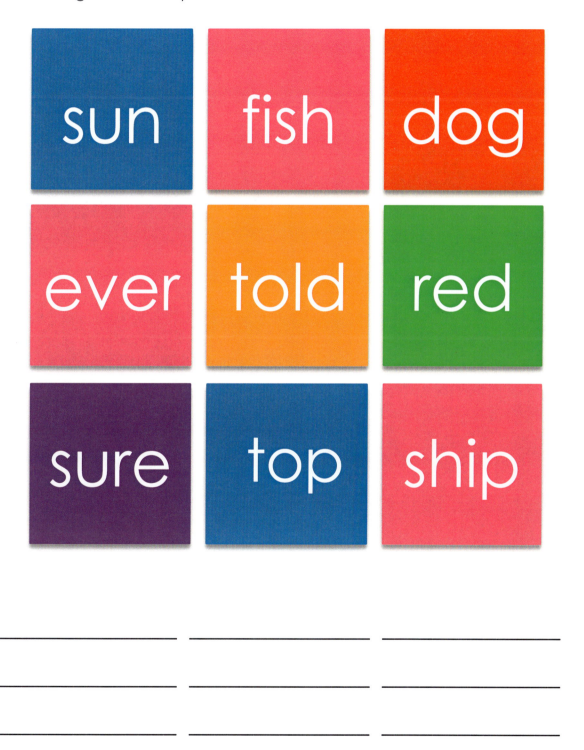

_____   _____   _____

_____   _____   _____

_____   _____   _____

Name the Color and Read the Word: Name the color of the square and then read the word in the square. Go as fast as you can! You can also read the word first then the color.
i.e. " blue sun, pink fish, red dog…"
Record your times below.

_____ _____ _____

_____ _____ _____

_____ _____ _____

1. **Read the Words:** "Say it slow." and "Say it fast." Don't move on to the next step until you have mastered the words.
2. **Name the Color and Read the Words:** Name the color first and then read the word quickly. i.e. "red best…"

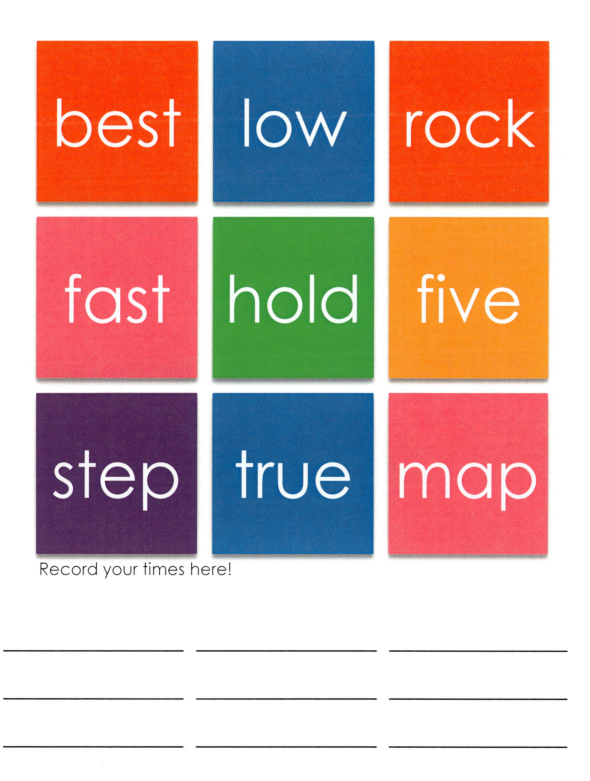

Record your times here!

_____   _____   _____

_____   _____   _____

_____   _____   _____

1. **Read the Words:**. "Say it slow." and "Say it fast." Don't move on to the next step until you have mastered the words.
2. **Name the Color and Read the Words:** Name the color first and then read the word quickly. i.e. "orange cold…"

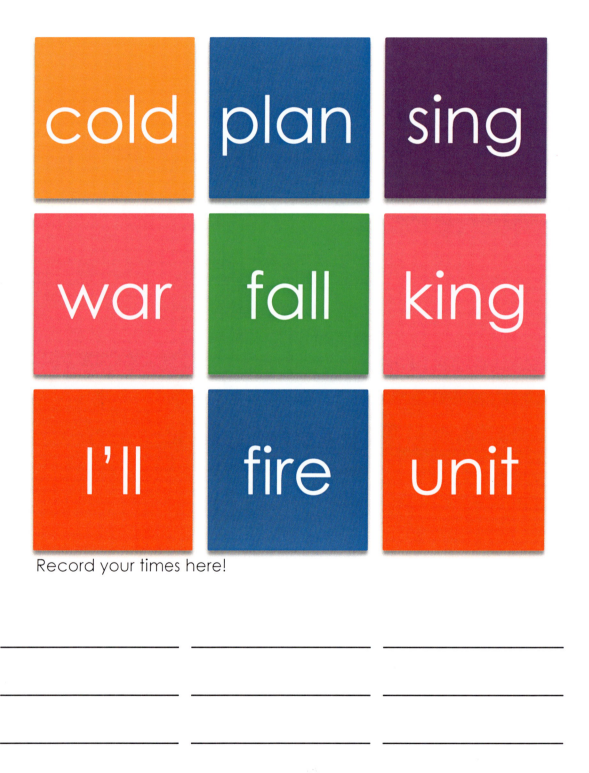

Record your times here!

_____ _____ _____

_____ _____ _____

_____ _____ _____

1. **Read the Words:**
   "Say it slow." and "Say it fast." Don't move on to the next step until you have mastered the words.
2. **Name the Color and Read the Words:** Name the color first and then read the word quickly.

body	color	area	mark
birds	room	knew	since
easy	order	door	short
hours	early	wind	table

_____ _____ _____

_____ _____ _____

_____ _____ _____

1. **Read the Words:**
   "Say it slow." and "Say it fast." Don't move on to the next step until you have mastered the words.
2. **Name the Color and Read the Words:** Name the color first and then read the word quickly.

music stand horse piece

didn't heard upon across

today wood seen black

farm field draw voice

_____ _____ _____

_____ _____ _____

_____ _____ _____

1. **Read the Words:**
   "Say it slow." and "Say it fast." Don't move on to the next step until you have mastered the words.
2. **Name the Color and Read the Words:** Name the color first and then read the word quickly.

north   cried   town   listen

space   waves   south

travel   usually   friends

better   whole   become

_____ _____ _____

_____ _____ _____

_____ _____ _____

1. **Read the Words:**
"Say it slow." and "Say it fast." Don't move on to the next step until you have mastered the words.
2. **Name the Color and Read the Words:** Name the color first and then read the word quickly.

certain   figure   ground

notice   pulled   money

slowly   vowel   passed

during   against toward

_____ _____ _____

_____ _____ _____

_____ _____ _____

1. **Read the Words:**
   "Say it slow." and "Say it fast." Don't move on to the next step until you have mastered the words.
2. **Name the Color and Read the Words:** Name the color first and then read the word quickly.

questions   happened

problem   measure

complete   remember

however   reached

products   covered

_____ _____ _____

_____ _____ _____

_____ _____ _____

1. **Read the Words:**
"Say it slow." and "Say it fast." Don't move on to the next step until you have mastered the words.
2. **Name the Color and Read the Words:** Name the color first and then read the word quickly.

several					pattern

himself					numeral

hundred					morning

_____ _____ _____

_____ _____ _____

_____ _____ _____

1. **Read the Words:** "Say it slow, Say it fast."

2. **Name the Color and Read the Word:** Name the color of the square and then read the word in the square. Go as fast as you can!

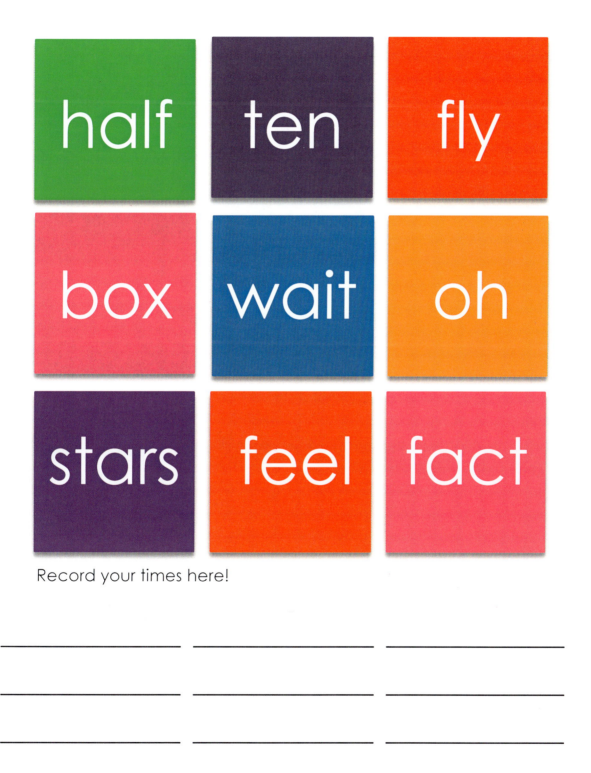

Record your times here!

_____   _____   _____

_____   _____   _____

_____   _____   _____

1. **Read the Words:** "Say it slow, Say it fast."

2. **Name the Color and Read the Word:** Name the color of the square and then read the word in the square. Go as fast as you can!

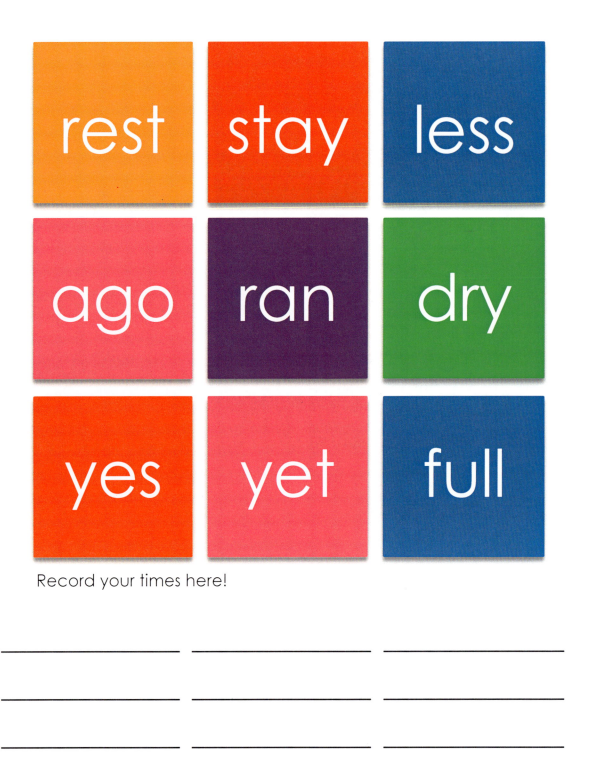

Record your times here!

_____   _____   _____

_____   _____   _____

_____   _____   _____

1. **Read the Words:** "Say it slow, Say it fast."

2. **Name the Color and Read the Word:** Name the color of the square and then read the word in the square. Go as fast as you can!

Record your times here!

_____   _____   _____

_____   _____   _____

_____   _____   _____

1. **Read the Words:**
   "Say it slow." and "Say it fast." Don't move on to the next step until you have mastered the words.
2. **Name the Color and Read the Words:** Name the color first and then read the word quickly.

done	street	week
road	ocean	base
gave	class	stood
verb	note	plane
front	inside	behind

_____ _____ _____

_____ _____ _____

_____ _____ _____

1. **Read the Words:**
   "Say it slow." and "Say it fast." Don't move on to the next step until you have mastered the words.
2. **Name the Color and Read the Words:** Name the color first and then read the word quickly.

built   noun   filled

circle   among   clear

heavy   object   deep

dark   check   shape

power   heat   bring

_____ _____ _____

_____ _____ _____

_____ _____ _____

1. **Read the Words:**
   "Say it slow." and "Say it fast." Don't move on to the next step until you have mastered the words.
2. **Name the Color and Read the Words:** Name the color first and then read the word quickly.

warm　system　cannot

force　inches　though

game　include　explain

boat　special　correct

round　green　material

_____　_____　_____

_____　_____　_____

_____　_____　_____

1. **Read the Words:**
   "Say it slow." and "Say it fast." Don't move on to the next step until you have mastered the words.
2. **Name the Color and Read the Words:** Name the color first and then read the word quickly.

island strong person

known surface shown

wheels English decided

course finally nothing

contain quickly building

_____ _____ _____

_____ _____ _____

_____ _____ _____

1. **Read the Words:**
   "Say it slow." and "Say it fast." Don't move on to the next step until you have mastered the words.
2. **Name the Color and Read the Words:** Name the color first and then read the word quickly.

brought	government
minutes	understand
produce	common
carefully	language
scientists	thousands
machine	equation

1. **Read the Words:** "Say it slow, Say it fast."

2. **Name the Color and Read the Word:** Name the color of the square and then read the word in the square. Go as fast as you can! You can also read the word first then the color.

_____   _____   _____

_____   _____   _____

_____   _____   _____

1. **Read the Words:** "Say it slow, Say it fast."

2. **Name the Color and Read the Word:** Name the color of the square and then read the word in the square. Go as fast as you can! You can also read the word first then the color.

_____   _____   _____

_____   _____   _____

_____   _____   _____

1. **Read the Words:**
   "Say it slow." and "Say it fast." Don't move on to the next step until you have mastered the words.
2. **Name the Color and Read the Words:** Name the color first and then read the word quickly.

can't	moon	mind	blue
wish	drop	main	kept
race	eggs	wide	arms
held	shall	soft	meet

_____ _____ _____

_____ _____ _____

_____ _____ _____

1. **Read the Words:**
   "Say it slow." and "Say it fast." Don't move on to the next step until you have mastered the words.
2. **Name the Color and Read the Words:** Name the color first and then read the word quickly.

grass	west	store	gone
edge	train	ready	paint
heart	third	drive	raised
I	can	read	fast

_____ _____ _____

_____ _____ _____

_____ _____ _____

1. **Read the Words:**
   "Say it slow." and "Say it fast." Don't move on to the next step until you have mastered the words.
2. **Name the Color and Read the Words:** Name the color first and then read the word quickly.

matter   subject   perhaps

square   region   syllables

cause   return   farmers

center   believe   divided

energy   dance   general

_____ _____ _____

_____ _____ _____

_____ _____ _____

1. **Read the Words:**
   "Say it slow." and "Say it fast." Don't move on to the next step until you have mastered the words.
2. **Name the Color and Read the Words:** Name the color first and then read the word quickly.

happy   Europe   length

record   reason   exercise

forest   brother   window

simple   beside   present

picked   written   summer

_____   _____   _____

_____   _____   _____

_____   _____   _____

1. **Read the Words:**
   "Say it slow." and "Say it fast." Don't move on to the next step until you have mastered the words.
2. **Name the Color and Read the Words:** Name the color first and then read the word quickly.

suddenly   probably

direction   winter

anything   interest

members   beautiful

developed   finished

difference   discovered

distance   million

_____ _____ _____

_____ _____ _____

_____ _____ _____

1. **Read the Words:**
   "Say it slow." and "Say it fast." Don't move on to the next step until you have mastered the words.
2. **Name the Color and Read the Words:** Name the color first and then read the word quickly.

describe   months

teacher   instruments

flowers   weather

clothes   syllables

whether   directions

represent   developed

paragraph   discovered

_____ _____ _____

_____ _____ _____

_____ _____ _____

Made in United States
North Haven, CT
19 October 2024